D1123150

THE BLACK & WHITE BOOK

THE BLACK & WHITE BOOK

TWO SIDES TO EVERY STORY

R. P. MOORE

POCKET BOOKS

New York   London   Toronto   Sydney   Singapore

POCKET BOOKS, a division of Simon & Schuster, Inc.
1230 Avenue of the Americas, New York, NY 10020

Copyright © 1999 by R. P. Moore

All rights reserved, including the right to reproduce
this book or portions thereof in any form whatsoever.
For information address Pocket Books, 1230 Avenue
of the Americas, New York, NY 10020

Library of Congress Cataloging-in-Publication Data

Moore, R. P.
   The black & white book / R. P. Moore.
      p. cm.
   ISBN 0-7434-1814-X
      1. Optimism. 2. Negativism. I. Title: Black and white book.
      II. Title

BF698.35.O57 M66 2001
158.1—dc21   00-069885

First Pocket Books hardcover printing May 2001

10 9 8 7 6 5 4 3 2 1

POCKET and colophon are registered trademarks of
Simon & Schuster, Inc.

Printed in the U.S.A.

Whether you swept through my life
for a few fleeting moments,
or whether you remain an integral part
of my life to this very day,
your contribution to this book
is immense. I thank you.

Introduction

I am no one in particular. I have no impressive credits to offer you. I'm not a doctor nor a psychic nor do I have a college degree. I don't even pray that the world be a better place. I am, however, someone interested in how things work. I am someone who watches and reflects. I am always in search of some common element that runs through everyone and everything whether at the grocery store or a memorial service or a wrestling match.

Absolutely everything I've encountered in my life has influenced the way I look at things. I've been shaped by fights in the schoolyard, reruns on TV and a Christian upbringing. I've learned from drinking and partying, crashing and burning. I've taken what works for me from twelve-step programs and self-help tapes and have been perfectly happy, then unhappy again. I've gone from being remarkably healthy to remarkably ill to remarkably healthy again. Whatever all of that makes me, I am.

I offer to you this collection of stories and circumstances. Some of them reflect my direct experience, some reflect the lives of others close to me at one time or another. Whatever the case, I identify with all of them. They form a collection of tremendous contrasts. And what greater contrast is there than placing self-indulgent hatred and disgust right beside profound love and understanding?

Acceptance is the single greatest concept I have ever incorporated into my life. Without it, I could not have authored this book. I at last accept my anger and my darkness, your fear and your hatred. I have found that it's only the resistance that makes these human conditions so painful. That's why I've just stopped trying to resist any feeling that overwhelms me. Including love.

THE BLACK & WHITE BOOK

And so it begins...

Everything sucks.

It's all good.

That Monica girl thinks she's so fucking hot. You know she does. She walks around with those haute half-moon eyes that just scream, "Go ahead. Just try to resist me." She's one of those that knows all the right people in all the right places. The tiniest little effort on her part gets, "Oh my God, Monica, that is soooo great. Hey! Everybody come over here!"

Well, sorry, but she is not Little Miss Perfect. And I refuse to contribute to that ever-swelling head of hers. Besides, she won't give me the time of day anyway. She will literally walk all the way around the office to avoid me. She knows I'm on to her. She knows I see her for the talentless hack that she is. She knows she won't hear "Oh my God, Monica, that is soooo great" from me. What would that gorged and fatted ego do then?

Oh, God. I am exhausted from the strain of maintaining this hatred. This is stupid. I'm giving this up.

Look, the truth is I've always liked Monica. Just like everybody else. Jealousy. It's that simple. It's me that has caused the problem here. It's me that has pushed her away and made her decide to avoid my unpleasantness. Or at the very least, it has been as much me as it has been her.

So, enough. I'm changing my mind. I already have. I have already started to not hold her beauty against her. I have already admitted that she is charming and witty. I am already noticing a difference.

I swear she's starting to see me differently as well. I've noticed in the past week that she has actually started passing by my desk. As a matter of fact, Tuesday she even came over and asked me where we keep the correction fluid.

From: JL - Senior Management Coordinator
Re: Staff meeting yesterday

* During yesterday's meeting, I found your comments to
be unprofessional and completely out of line.

* I find your ignorance appalling and advise against
further such incidents.

* I further indicate to you that our so-called 'bunch
of slackers' has been placed in the unfair position of
correcting YOUR asinine mistakes.

* Bite me.

From: Jim in Management
Re: Yesterday's meeting

So things got a little heated yesterday at the staff
meeting. I can see why you got upset. Things haven't
been running real smoothly lately.

I hope you can see the whole picture, though. We're
spending a lot of time redoing things. That's where I
need your help. Just for the next few weeks, could you
double-check the files before they come to us? Things
have to be done so quickly around here that it's real
easy to overlook some of the smaller things.

Let's first see if that solves any problems. And please
bring any issues to me as soon as they come up. The
rest of the staff gets a bit discouraged when they hear
ONLY our negativity.

Thanks!

Jim

I'm the one that asks why you were fifteen minutes late.

I'm the one that comes running up with a two-day project due at 5:00.

I'm the one that makes you go back and do the whole damn thing again because it's just not what we had in mind.

I'm the one that gives you "the look" when you're slacking off.

I'm the one that's never around when you're looking for me.

I'm the one that takes two-hour lunches but lets you have it for taking more than your hour for the past few days.

I'm the one that dresses goofy.

I'm the one that can afford all the latest styles.

I'm the one that just sits and talks on the phone all day.

I'm the one that yells and screams and tells everybody they're insane.

I'm the one that calls you in the middle of dinner and wants to know where that yellow file is. You know, the one from this morning.

I'm the one that runs your life every day, all week long.

Maybe I really like you.

Maybe I'm just doing what *my* bosses want me to do.

Maybe I *do* consider that you have kids who want Daddy to get home.

Maybe I'm as scared as you are.

Maybe I wonder if you have it better than I do.

Maybe I wish everybody loved their job as much as I do.

Maybe the thought never even crossed my mind that you are a loser just because you live in a studio apartment and I have a three bedroom house.

Maybe I question whether I said the right thing to you.

Maybe I fucked up.

Maybe I hope you'll take over one day.

Maybe I understand how unfulfilling this job is for you and hope you find something really cool.

Maybe I don't make as much as you think I do. And what if I did?

It was my last interview for this job. Charles had already proven himself to be an uptight, busybody know-it-all. He even made this big deal the first time we met about me taking some stupid dime I found in the chair I was sitting in. I *said* he could have it! Geez!!

I had already given three flawless presentations to him over the past five unemployed weeks. Each time he looked to be really pleased. And I swear I caught him nodding in agreement a few times. "Good. Very creative," he'd say. Then inevitably I'd hear, "Not quite what we're looking for, though. You can try again if you like."

What??? If it's good and creative what's the freakin' problem??? Okay, so I was fresh out of college. And so I had no practical experience yet. But if it's *good* . . . ?

It was my last interview for this job because I flat out told him it was. I explained that I had offered numerous "good" and "very creative" approaches and I would have no choice but to invest my energy elsewhere if this final offering didn't do it for him.

No longer sure I wanted to work for this impossible man, I proceeded to give it one last shot and removed my presentation boards from the briefcase. Before I could even open my mouth, Charles walked over, shuffled through the boards, looked at me with his unreadable face, and said, "Excellent. Welcome to the company."

Charles turned away a moment in silence before looking at me again. "I'd pretty much decided on you the first day, you know."

Um, no I did not know!! Was this guy jerking me around or what?? After five weeks without a job, the grocery store was starting to be about as accessible as a five-star restaurant!

"Charles," I said, my tone weird with exhilaration and confusion—

—Charles, noting my frustration, did me the great favor of interrupting. "I put that dime in the chair that first day," he said gently and with an empathy I had not recognized in him before. "You were on your way out of the building when I asked if you had taken it. Very awkward. Very easy to blow off. After all, it's only a dime. You said you'd taken it and even offered it back. Thanks."

He apologized for taking so much of my time over the past weeks. He said he didn't know it was so valuable to me. After all, it's only five weeks. It turns out that although he liked my stuff, it had taken this long for him to convince the others. I think he actually wished he could offer back my time. I found that I got back far more than that.

With multiple projects going on every week, it became vital to the workplace that I stand up and say, "We have got to make a decision *today* and move on to the next thing." Without that unemployed five week training period, I'd have never been able to take that stand. And because of a dime, they listened.

In college, a bunch of my friends, unlike me, were superb athletes. They'd joke around about my thin frame and it kinda bothered me, but not enough to do anything about it.

One day I was helping one of my jock friends move. Todd was stacking boxes in the truck when he remembered this plant he had inside, so I ran in to get it. I went to pick it up. It wouldn't budge. I tried again. Not an inch. After about four tries, I was completely out of breath. And that's when Todd came in. He gave me a half-concerned, half-amused look that cut through me like a chainsaw. Then he went over and just yanked that plant up like it was a trash bag. That did it! I changed my mind. Never would one of my best friends see me as less than equal. I was gonna work out!

And I did. I gave myself 100 percent to maximum muscle mass programs and high protein meals and weight gain supplements. Slowly, it worked! It took about eighteen months, but I was fuckin' buffed, man!

Oh, wow! Every now and then I'd walk past a window and I couldn't believe how incredible I looked! And I figured, "Hey, I've got it, might as well show it!" Finally! I was able to go buy tank tops and shirts with the sleeves ripped out! Shoot, when you look this fuckin' good, you might as well strut, right?

By now Todd was nowhere near as solid as me. That's probably why he stopped hangin' with me. That whole group got all jealous and started flaking on me. Hey, you know what? It doesn't matter. I'm doin' what's workin' and that's that. Nothin's gonna stand in my way now!

Having Todd see me as an equal was so important to me, I made the decision not to be scrawny anymore. I set my sights on working out and gaining muscle and that's exactly what I did.

It was an extremely fulfilling experience. For years I always thought, "Oh, I just don't have the frame" or "I'm just not the athletic type." I rearranged my thinking and rose above every barrier I had convinced myself was there. YES!!! I don't think anything is more empowering than a radical new choice.

Somewhere along the way, something else changed, though. I stopped focusing on the original goal, which was to feel one with my friends, and started looking only at the by-product of my attempt to get there. It became all about having bigger and better flesh than everyone else. It became all about making sure everyone looked at my bigger and better flesh. It became about my flesh and how impressed you were with it.

I lost my friends. Actually, more truthfully, they lost me. I left them behind. Making sure I blew everyone away became far more important than them. I've come to find out, however, that without anyone to share with, my big goals and big dreams and big accomplishments don't blow anybody away. Especially me.

I've
gained
15 pounds
in the *last*
month!!

What about You has not changed?

I was watching one of those daytime talk shows a while back and there were all these people that had undergone sex change operations or were about to. These people make me sick! I don't think I've ever heard one of these freaks not use the line, "I'm a woman trapped in a man's body," or vice versa. God! What a crock of shit!

The idea that somebody's "trapped" in the wrong body is just screwed up. That's the way you were born and that's the way God intended it! Stop trying to mess around with the natural perfection of things. I guaran-fucking-tee you that you get the operation and still feel all wrong because you are and you know it!

In recent years, physical enhancement surgery has become far, far less taboo. Face-lifts, breast augmentations, liposuction are all household words. Before this minor revolution took place, I regarded altering the body in any way a less-than-Godly decision. As more people began to have these procedures, I decided differently. I mean, hey, our bodies are not who we are, right? If slicing, dicing, and tucking bring you happiness and fulfillment, go for it.

The idea of gender change always stopped me in my tracks. I was watching a daytime talk show on the topic and the accusations and opinions were getting rather heated. My auto-prejudger had already determined long ago that the desire to change gender did not come from God, so they should not even try to make that point. Then a moment of clarity. A friend of mine, who was Caucasian, had begun dating a black guy. I remember so many people in town freaking out and saying God did not intend for races to intermix—it was a sin against nature. All I could see were two people that felt drawn to each other. I went with my heart on this one despite those opinions.

I changed my mind right then and there. I have no idea what God would have you do. I have no idea what you came into this realm to demonstrate to the rest of us. I have no idea what your soul is specifically instructing you to do for whatever purpose it might serve. I want you to follow your calling. That way, I feel free enough to follow mine.

"Oh, what **is** this world coming to? Yesterday I was walking down the sidewalk and standing there talking to a very nice gentleman was this **dreadful** young man. He was one of those with all the **pierced** body parts and he had absolutely **disfigured** his body from head to toe with these **horrible** tattoos!

I didn't catch anything else, but as I walked by, I heard him to persuade the other one that, **and** I quote, '. . . yeah, but guilt's not all that important, dude . . .'

Oh! What **is** this world coming to? "

Guilt is not all that important.

SURGEON GENERAL'S WARNING: Smoking Causes Lung Cancer, Heart Disease, Emphysema, And May Complicate Pregnancy.

Are you choosing Love in this moment?

I'm the one that just stands against the wall smoking a cigarette.

I'm the one that rarely talks to anyone.

I'm the one that catches your eye the moment you walk in the bar.

I'm the one that looks like such an asshole.

I'm the one who would certainly tell you to fuck off.

I'm the one your friends say is checking you out, but you know better.

I'm the one that, if you could break that ice away, would show you the time of your life.

I'm just a whore.

I'm the one that would use you and spit you out like four-hour gum.

I'm the one you better not mess with.

Maybe you've got me all wrong.

Maybe I was hoping you'd be here.

Maybe I know what you're thinking and couldn't blame you a bit.

Maybe I think you're really beautiful.

Maybe there's just too much I would have to explain.

Maybe we should get out of here.

Maybe I'm sure you'd tell me to fuck off.

Maybe I think you're too caring to handle a one–night stand.

Maybe I'm too sensitive and caring to handle a one–night stand.

Maybe I'm the one.

Maybe I wouldn't hold it against you for not speaking to me until now.

I met this guy in a bar. The most beautiful man I'd ever laid eyes on. We talked for hours. He said he was tired of how everybody in bars just wants to go home and get laid. He told me some of his most personal secrets. I told him some of mine. I gave him my number. We made plans for him to come by my place the next afternoon. He never showed up.

Asshole . . . just like everybody else.

The guy . . . that I met in the bar . . . I just couldn't stop thinking about him. Even though he flaked on me, I refuse to believe he was an asshole. When I pull back and look at things from a higher place, I realize it was fear. He was afraid of something. He was simply *afraid*. Afraid of his feelings for me. Afraid to tell me something about himself. Or maybe he was afraid the entire time at the bar and just pretended to like me because he didn't know what else to do.

I hope he knows we're all afraid of things. I hope he knows it's really okay. After all, I only want the truth. I want only love.

The rich get richer.

What resources have you been given to expand upon?

Everybody thinks I make tons of money and suggest that I should be living it up. Who the hell are they to even *think* they know my financial situation? Who are they to think they can tell me how to spend what I *do* have? Money doesn't grow on trees, you know. It takes a lot of work to build up even the least little bit. And what if I got sick and couldn't work anymore? Or what if my house burned down? Or what if the price of everything triples by the time I'm sixty-five? And what if there's not Social Security anymore? Then what?

I have this friend that spends every dime he makes. He buys the latest clothes, has to have a new car every two or three years or he'll just die, takes his dates to these overpriced restaurants, and lives in this high-rise apartment that's too big for him. What a fool. What's he going to do thirty years from now when he's a burnt-out, over-the-hill salesman that nobody wants to buy from anymore? Knock on my door, probably.

I make lots of money. I do. I've always thought that was unacceptable. There was always this idea that making money made me bad. And saving money, now that made me a hypocrite or a selfish bastard. I'm starting to see how those ideas just aren't true.

Everyday of my life I am grateful for the opportunities I have been given. I'm grateful for the opportunities I've been wise enough to accept, too. Something inside me tells me to prepare. For what I don't even know. Maybe I'll have a kid. And I'm able to send that kid to a great college. Maybe that kid will discover the cure for some strange disease. Or maybe I'll just give my kids the gift of not being a burden on them.

I think there's something to be said for living a simple life, too. I need very little, therefore, I am *in need* very little. And it just seems to work out that the less I need, the more I have. I'm pleased with myself. I feel responsible. I feel wise.

If a financial guy were to make a list of my assets, he'd come up with nothing. I was completely fucked over by a bad business deal years ago and I've been struggling to get back ever since. I'm sure everybody thinks I'm totally loaded because of where I live, what I drive, and what I wear. The truth is, I have a friend in real estate that lets me stay in this penthouse for almost nothing *but* can tell me to hit the road at anytime. I'm trapped in the lease game with cars, and I shuffle through piles of second-rate crap at discount stores.

I know this guy that has got to make more money in a week than I make all month. This jerk spends all day on the phone shuffling his stocks around then goes home to some bleak studio apartment he's had for ten years because it's rent controlled and "all he needs." God, what a fool! I'm the one that should be making all that cash! I'm the one that wants to live!!

I've got to admit, I'm proud of myself. I had every reason to throw in the towel forever, but I didn't. I took responsibility for not only my financial mistakes, but someone else's, too. Oh, and I stopped asking "Why." Even with my mistakes, I have always felt I deserved the best this life has to offer and somehow I have it!

On paper it may look like I don't have a whole lot, but facts don't tell it straight, baby. To me, when you can say, "I love where I live" and "My car always starts" and "I love the way I look" and "I have a great life" what else could you possibly need? I have everything I want right now this instant. And when your butt's against the wall, you finally learn to live right now.

For months and months and months I tried to catch your eye; almost every day for the greater part of a year. Your face was beautiful, but I knew you had to be a total bitch because you kept your lips closed tightly and looked only to the floor. You knew goddamn well I was looking your way. **YOU KNEW IT!! God what a bitch!** I approached you a few times. You replied courteously, even cheerfully, then went back to your closed-off world almost instantly.

I think it was the day you spotted me in my brand new car that you decided you would give me a chance. Whatever. It didn't matter. Here you were, the object of my desire, finally giving me the time of day. At last I felt like you would go out with me. I wish you hadn't.

I hate you! I was kind to you! I showed you respect! I, unlike the others you made reference to, was not out to only get a piece. Sure, I desired you. I had every intent to get it on with you. WITH YOU, not despite you. That's why I waited. I respected the feelings you said you had. **BIG MISTAKE!** I should've just fucked you the first night and gotten it over with!

You took everything I offered you and gave **NOTHING!** You took my respect and gave none in return. You made promises you had no intention of keeping. You didn't want to talk or be emotionally intimate. You made sure that somehow, some way, there would always be others around to make sure we didn't get close. When I tried to tell you how I felt, you cut me off midsentence. Get lost.

I have always found you to be beautiful. I have offered myself to you over and over. I have come to realize, however, you are not ready for such all-encompassing love. You must think it's too good to be true, therefore you are not ready to receive it.

I don't care what you say or do, I can feel you calling to me. I can feel how much you appreciate me. I can feel how deep runs our connection. I am so sorry you were hurt. I am so sorry you believe you cannot be loved and admired and respected for who you really are in your most private moments. I love you. It's just that simple. I want so much for that to dawn on you.

It is so unfortunate that the fear you cling to is holding not only you back, but me as well. I cannot sit and wait with your fear. My soul calls me forward and beyond it. How long will you remain in that dark closet, so sure that everything is not okay? How long will you remain unaware of how perfect and beautiful and free you actually are? And will you use my moving on as further proof that no one cares? Probably. Then one day, I assure you, you will decide that there *has* to be another way of looking at things. To be there with you on that day, at that brilliant moment. To be near you and a part of your life when you become everything you ever wanted to be.

I'm already there. I already see everything you are.

In this booming metropolis,

You can't make eye contact
with anyone on the street
unless you know them,

*You can't make eye contact
with anyone at a bar
unless you want to have sex with them,*

YOU CAN'T MAKE EYE CONTACT
WITH ANYONE AT THE GYM
UNLESS THEY NEED A SPOT,

But on the **hiking trail,**
you can make
all sorts of eye contact
and say "Hi" and say
"Beautiful morning, isn't it?"
and smile and wave!

What are you supposed to do with an entire population of two-faced
assholes like that?

Go hiking.

I ran into my neighbors on the elevator and came to learn that they are actors. I never watch whatever it is they're on, so if they weren't my neighbors, I'd walk right over them if they were lying naked in the street. However, since our introduction, anytime I hold the elevator for them, they flash their big Hollywood smiles and chirp, "Oh, no, we'll take the stairs!" What's up with *that*? I mean, it happens all the time! I encounter one or both of them in the lobby getting the mail. I hold the elevator; they take the stairs. We leave our apartments at the same time. The stairs. They have groceries. Stairs. What wretched event could possibly take place in the elevator with me? Do they fear I'll ask for their autographs? Are they afraid I'll try to get into "the movies"? Fine! Screw 'em!

The other day, the guy came out of his apartment dragging two very heavy garbage bags. This time I was certain he'd need the elevator. "Uuuhh, no. Thanks though," he said as he reached for the stairwell door. I didn't even question it at this point and headed down to the lobby. On the way, I remembered some papers I'd left in the apartment, so I had to come right back up again. Yep. There he was. Standing there with the garbage bags waiting for the elevator. Asshole jerk.

So my neighbors do not wish to ride the elevator with me. The truth is that they are perfectly free not to. They are perfectly entitled to do exactly as they feel no matter what I think. Hooray for them for living out their choices despite what society has deemed polite or nice or "the right thing to do in a situation like that."

Maybe they are indeed afraid. Maybe they think I'm a geek. Maybe they don't particularly like me. Maybe their choice is out of a limiting belief that has no basis in reality. Would it serve at all for me to give them the "evil eye" or emit the "guilt ray"? I feel that would only serve to justify in their minds that people are indeed out to get them, or are geeks, or unlikable and it's better to steer clear.

Everyone is not going to do what I think they should do. Many, many people will prefer to walk the other way. I'm fine with that idea. Sometimes I need to walk the other way, too.

This
book
sucks!

Perhaps this is not specifically for you.

My father often took our family on business trips with him. We'd frequently see a friend of his that was nice and all, but he never made any big impression on me personally. Until I learned he had a pacemaker. Through my ten-year-old eyes, he seemed way too young to have a pacemaker. And it was sort of creepy to me in those technological dark ages to think of some mechanism in charge of his life. It's still sort of creepy if you think about it.

Then I learned that he had to have a second one put in. Then a third. Gosh, what a nightmare for this guy.

Then I learned that he was unable to tolerate any form of anesthesia. Each surgery, the doctor had come to his home, sliced him open, and inserted the pacemakers while he sat in some chair he thought was really comfortable.

The idea of a normal, everyday-kinda-guy enduring surgery after surgery while sitting in a chair looking at the molding on the ceiling always stuck with me. It was instant proof to me that we can do anything. And I still believe that.

As my life progressed, I began experiencing enough pain, through just migraines and emotional turmoil, to start meditating. I began to discover that if I could really and truly be in the moment, there was no pain. It took a while to get still enough and quiet enough. Then it took a while to start sensing that there's something beyond this ever-chatting brain. Then it took a while to melt into that "something" or that "nothing." Finally I learned how to feel no pain and even ultimate bliss (without a hangover).

I don't think I'm ready to have my appendix removed with meditation as my anesthesia, nor do I want that. I don't even meditate a headache away if I'm within five miles of an aspirin. I do meditate when I'm not happy or confused or need to put on the brakes. That's most everyday.

Poor Christopher Reeve. So tragic. How can it be that such a wise and courageous man should have his potential cut short and be left confined and unable to function as a normal human being?

How can it be that it is so difficult to recognize the profound wisdom and courage normal functioning human beings offer?

Years ago, I had a roommate named Jaime. Jaime was a "niceguy." He even said so himself. "Hey, I'm just a nice guy." You know the type. They do what everybody wants them to do and they overcompensate so everybody they know will like them. Because, hey, they're nice. He was the ideal roommate, I must say. Always paid the rent two days early, let me furnish the apartment in whatever way I chose. And he never ate my groceries. Once Jaime drove thirty-two miles into the next county to take a friend to a party that he wasn't even invited to. How nice of Jaime helping a friend in need like that.

One day I walked by Jaime's room and saw him with a video cartridge, the tape pulled out and on the table in front of him. He seemed to be scraping up and down the tape with a razor blade. He was a novice photographer so I figured he knew what he was doing.

That night I went to a friend's place and we decided to rent a movie. As we walked into the video store, there was Jaime at the front counter pointing his finger in the clerk's face and demanding, "Where's the manager? Get me the manager. That tape is totally fucked up and you guys are gonna give me my money back. Get me the manager!" Nice.

I certainly grew up with the idea that it was not okay to be angry. Yet, I was. No matter what I did, no matter how "good" I wanted to be, something would come along and make me angry. For the longest time I looked at Jaime with jealousy. I wondered how on earth anyone could be that giving and that easy all the time. Then I was shown that he, too, was angry. He simply chose to fuck over impersonal franchises and institutions. What a perfect messenger he was for me. He convinced me that not only do we all have anger, but that it must be and will be expressed. He also showed me exactly what I did not want to be. And do not mistake that statement as a put-down. Someone along our way *must* show us what we do not want to be. How else will we know what we *do* want instead?

I no longer swallow my anger. I've learned that, if you do, it always comes right back up. And at the worst time and in the worst way. If something pisses me off, I try to let it out right then and there. That way, there is no mistake as to what I'm angry about. There is no resentment brewing inside. There is no need to devise a plan to get back at anyone. There is no anger anymore. (Until the next time.)

I've had it with you. I HAVE **HAD IT!** I have hung in there with you longer than I've hung with anyone in my adult life. **And for what?!!** Have I been in some sort of delusional state? You offer me absolutely nothing anymore! It seems I have spent more time forgiving and letting bygones be bygones than receiving any kind of joy from you at all.

When I need to talk, you don't have time for it. Oh, sure, you'll fit me in while you're waiting for somebody else to call. I can't count the times your goddamn call-waiting has made you forget I was even alive. Not to mention on **the other line!**

WILL YOU **EVER** GROW UP???

I hate you. It's that simple. You are so completely selfish I could vomit at the thought of you. Get the hell outta my life!

This is so long overdue. There's been a branch in the road for such a long time. We can't hold on to each other anymore. It's just going to hurt more and more the further we advance. And besides, it's only temporary.

Isn't the human condition a strange thing? We have things like priorities and choices and hopes and fears and goals. Things that really don't matter, but things we have to use unless we want to be stagnant. And neither of us want that.

Go. Go on along your way. Please, for God's sake, go. Please be exactly who you are. Please be exactly who you want to be. You don't need my permission. I don't have to like it.

Do you know how much respect I have for you in this moment? As ironic as it sounds, my soul is literally alive with joy because you are leaving me. You have made the perfect, right decision for yourself. And, therefore, for me. And, therefore, for everyone.

This is a cruel world.
All I see is hatred and anger!
Poverty and injustice!

See something else.

Somebody broke into my car last night. What else can happen? It has been nothing but a nightmare since I moved to L.A. I feel almost certain they're gonna fire me at work. I'm just not giving them what they want. Whatever that is. And that goddamn dog downstairs never stops barking!

I had to make this move. I mean, I HAD to get away from Greg, but GOD I wish there were somebody here. Just somebody that I could talk to. Everybody in this fucking city is so closed-off! They look at you like you're a moron if you say HI. Fuck 'em all. This was probably all a big mistake.

This city's just too big for me. My old boss said I wouldn't make it here. Now I know he was right. This place is chewing me up and spitting me out like so many others. I can FEEL it.

As it turned out, it was never L.A.'s intent to chew me up or spit me out. Instead, it paved a way for me to leave a terrible relationship. It paved the way for me to come and be with myself and see the perfection in that terrible relationship. It became the place where I would discover what I am capable of and who I am. It demonstrated to me how to live one instant at a time. A rich and full life did not begin until I took the risk of following my heart and made the move to the big city. L.A. brought me to my knees then said, "Okay, now, get up and do it right this time."

I thought I would never make a friend here. But I have friends here. I learned to walk up and just start talking to those I feel drawn toward. It seems a bunch of us have been waiting for just that.

L.A. has literally been the City of Angels for me. Some are angels of deliverance, some are angels of death, a few are angels of mercy, and all are angels in disguise.

Only darkness surrounds me.

Open your eyes.

Years ago I bought a '59 Cadillac. I took it to a body shop out of the county to have it restored as it cost considerably less there. They took my car apart, sold the parts to an underground operation, and skipped town. I was out thousands of dollars.

The incident paid my income taxes for two years.

After years of being single, I finally found a woman I fell in love with. It came just at the right time, too, because my career was totally bumming me out and I didn't know what to do. This new light on the horizon could maybe answer some questions about my future.

It had been so long since I had found someone else that I could relate to and enjoyed being with all the time and did not want gone after we did it. This was a dream come true! I even gave up smoking for her, something I never thought I could do!

After several months she left for a guy that smoked.

Chicks sucking and all, I decided it was time to do something to get me rich and happy. I had sat around not accomplishing a goddamn thing for way too long. I'd write a novel! Yeah! I'd write a thinly disguised tale about that hate-filled wench. I'd use every little annoying, bitchy, whiny thing she did. And I'd make her do every evil thing I know she really wanted to but never would.

Okay, so it's not published yet. But I did that broad up real good!

I decided I needed something to take my mind off my money problems. I deduced that a relationship would do nicely. Inherently a powerful being and convinced that this was exactly what I needed, I was able to draw a relationship to me.

The relationship rapidly started to fail. She was not happy. She decided that she must get out, but she would have to devise a way to end this thing without saying, "I want out." She calculated that since I was addicted to smoking and could not stop, she'd use that as the thing that was "coming between us." She even convinced herself that it indeed was.

I had devised this plan that a relationship would divert my attention from my financial woes. I would quit smoking, that would solve this problem and my well-laid scheme could continue as calculated.

Then everything took a completely unforeseen turn as she met someone that she truly wanted to be with. He smoked. I saw them together. She was embarrassed. I felt betrayed. "We had a plan! What about the plan???"

A strong wind had swept through and blown the blueprints from my clutching hands. Now I had no plan and everything felt like a mess.

Then something very strange happened. I began to feel a creative urging. I was feeling a need to write down everything that had happened. I didn't know why I felt this way, I just did. So I began to write. It was deeply fulfilling.

I at last finished this truly inspired work. Every person that read it was likewise inspired and deeply moved. I have even looked into getting this novel published. I can't tell you if it will be or if it won't.

I can tell you that it helped me move beyond a broken heart. I can tell you that this inspired writing has inspired others. I can tell you that I never realized I had so much potential. And I never planned on any of that.

There are words in this book that don't even exist! I've counted at least two hundred and fifty sentences that end with prepositions! There is no consistency in line spacing and this type is hard to read!

Focus on whatever you like.

No matter what I've done
to avoid it, I have always
been led right back
to the horrific demands
of a fast-paced corporation!

Okay, so I love it.

I was leaving for this convention in St. Louis in an hour and a half. I was packing when I realized that I would have two major dinners to go to. I only had one jacket that I was sure was okay and another one that *might* do, but it smelled like the hall closet. You know, like Grandma.

I figured I had just enough time to run to the store down the street and grab something. At least I'd know it was made in this decade. I ran down there and saw the perfect one right away. I yanked it off the hanger and tried it on. Yeah, yeah, looked good to me. I had to get outta there.

So I got home with just enough time to finish packing and hit the road. I took the jacket from the bag and noticed it had one of those magnetic anti-theft tags on it. Crap. I figured I'd snap the thing off with the pliers. Hey, I'm strong and all, but this thing wouldn't come off. I had the pliers, the hammer, vice grips, and an ice pick at this fuckin' tag. I finally dug out my dremel set and sawed the thing off.

After everything I put that jacket through, I thought I better look at it in the mirror and make sure it was okay. What the hell happened? The jacket was in fine shape, but it was like ten sizes too big! It looked fine in the store. I thought. I don't know, I was in a hurry! Needless to say, I went to the party smelling like Grandma.

When I was on the plane, I started thinking about the whole jacket thing. I wish I had a video, man. I was hammerin' that jacket and sawin' on it . . . the only thing I needed was a fuckin' safety helmet. I started laughing right there on the plane. I think the guy next to me thought I was nuts.

Ya know, it's pretty cool to be able to just decide to go buy a jacket. Gosh, I think back to a few years ago when I would've had to save and budget and stay at home on weekends if I needed a jacket or anything like that. Pretty cool.

I went from Corporate Account Executive
to selling flowers from a cart in the mall.

I went from being stressed out, miserable, and tied-down
to being creative, content, and free.

Several years ago, I lost my job. My entire department was deemed unprofitable to the company and terminated. I was terribly frightened. Nothing like this had ever happened to me before.

I began drawing unemployment. I started instantly trying to find a position in a company somewhere. Week after week, I got nowhere. I finally had to move in with a friend until I could get back on my feet.

Somewhere along the way, something happened. I didn't want to go look for a job. It started suiting me just fine to live in a small room in someone else's home. I was okay with not being able to pay the insurance on my car. I even became perfectly content with letting my car be repossessed and getting a clunker.

What was happening to me? I had never been this way at all! I was managing an entire staff of people before this mess I was in! But I just could not make myself get out of this rut. I'd go to job interviews and say under my breath, "Don't give me this job, don't give me this job, don't give me this job . . ." No one ever gave me the job.

One day I was looking through the books on my friend's shelf and I came across one entitled *Numerology*. I began to read through it. This book outlined an entire system of mapping out a person's life! With a little math, you could figure out where you were going, where you were now, and look at where you had been! I calculated everything just the way it instructed.

When I looked back upon my life, it completely corresponded with everything numerology was showing me. And most important, it was indicating that at this particular period in my life, I was to work as little as possible. It showed that this was a time to reflect and look within. I was so relieved. Not only did this explain what was going on, but it demonstrated in writing that this was all temporary. Whew.

Numerology came into my life to set me free right when I needed it. It gave me good reasons to believe there's more at work than I could ever conceive. It showed me that there's a time and place for everything. Even numerology.

I've gone to at least six auditions a week for the last nine years.

Nothing.

I've sent out promo packages every six months for the last nine years.

Nothing.

I've spent everything I've made in the last nine years on landing a part.

Nothing.

My husband left me because he just doesn't understand and I'm living in my car. I had to buy a costume for an audition so I haven't eaten in the last couple days, but I'll get that role, you just watch! I made up my mind years ago that I was going to do this and goddammit I will!

I will!   I will!   I will!

Who are you doing this for?

"The ideas
in this book
are stupid
and impractical!"

The way to happiness is completely unaffected by your opinions.

. . . and crystals are very effective
for removing deadened energy
from the cracks and corners
of your living space . . .

Oh, please. Get out the vacuum cleaner and get busy. You'll feel better.

MONDAY P.M. — Jesus Christ! What was I thinking?!! I got caught up in this random moment of holiday cheer and agreed to give a dinner party. In four days! Hey, I work, you know. I have to go to the gym everyday. I have another party I'm supposed to go to tomorrow night. Oh, God! I still have to shop for gifts that must be sent out by Friday. This is crazy. I think I better back out of this. But I really, really want to do it.

TUESDAY P.M. — Crap! Of all days to have to work late. This place is a wreck! I don't have any time to go to the gym, either. Oh, man, it's gonna take me all night tomorrow night just to get this place in order. And it doesn't look like Christmas at all. It's gotta look like Christmas. It's Christmas, for Christ's sake. I gotta get dressed. This party's in an hour. God! This shirt's all wrinkled!

WEDNESDAY P.M. — Okay, just forget the gym. I'll just be a big fat pig. Everybody else is at Christmas. Let's see, just start picking up the wrapping paper in the corner . . . WAIT! The gifts I have to send out! All right, I'll run to the store and grab some things — you know the lines are gonna be a mile long — and get some decorations for this place while you're at it. And I think you're out of paper towels, too. Maybe I should write all this down. Just go.

THURSDAY P.M. — God! This place is a wreck! Okay, just start picking up the wrapping paper in the corner over there. Maybe I should run the dishwasher while I'm cleaning. Actually, maybe I should go get all the groceries while the dishwasher's running. Yeah.

- - - - - - - - - - - - - - - -

Oh, that cost waaay too much. Shut up and just put everything away. No, wait, just leave it there. Except for the cold stuff. You've got to get the bathrooms cleaned up. You idiot, you better start the turkey . . . like now. Then clean. And baste. And decorate. And polish silverware.

FRIDAY P.M. — Get . . . this . . . stupid . . . coat off! Alright, get the decorations up. Wait. Where's the tape? I know I have tape.

- - - - - - - - - - - - - -

There it is!

- - - - - - - - - - - - - -

That'll just have to do. Set the table. No, get in the shower and get ready first.

- - - - - - - - - - - - - -

Where's that other bowl? Don't forget to turn the stereo on. What's on this fork?

- - - - - - - - - - - - - -

"Hi! Come on in. No, I said seven o'clock, but that's fine! Let me turn the music on. You can _____ watch me _____ while I'm cooking."

SATURDAY A.M. — That was one of the most perfect evenings of my life. Yes, a simple little dinner party. There's something that happens to your place when you open it to others. It makes absolutely everything come to life. That chair in the corner that no one ever sits in, someone sits in. That picture on the mantel that has completely blended into the background after being there so long, someone holds in their hand and really looks at it. The back burners on the stove get to do something for a change.

It is often said that the best gifts are the ones you make yourself. My one goal was to create a beautiful evening and give it. In my mind I could *see* the people, I could *taste* the food, I could *hear* the music, and I could *feel* the energy. It was all so clear to me, that I had to bring it to life. Would you believe that amid all the chaos leading up to that night, I was peaceful deep inside? I wanted to do this.

Thank you. Thank you for holding your vision close and making it happen. Thank you for not deciding it wasn't worth it. Thank you for being prosperous enough to extend yourself far and wide. Thank you for knowing who you are.

THE FOLLOWING MONDAY A.M. — GOD! I just talked to Terri for almost an hour and she didn't even mention the fact that I had her and Jim over for dinner the other night! Ummm, hello? Remember me? I spent a whole week cooking and cleaning and spending more money than I should have for you guys. Remember?

So what's the deal? Did they think it was stupid? Or just kinda cute? Did they think I was trying to be a show-off? Were they pissed off because the conversation got a little racy for a while? WHAT'S THE DEAL??!!!

Goddamn! See if I ever invite either one of them over again.

THAT MONDAY P.M.—Maybe I'm missing something, but I'm sorry, I don't get it. It was my purest intent to share joy and good feelings. The idea that someone would misconstrue that is disturbing. However, I have to let it go. I must.

It's got to be okay that someone did not enjoy themselves. It's got to be okay if someone thinks I'm an arrogant ass. It has to be all right if someone wants to exchange the gift I gave them. It has to be fine if someone thought I made a pathetic attempt.

I always go back to a line from *A Course in Miracles* that says, "Only the truth is true and nothing else is true." I gave because I genuinely wanted to. Perhaps I have not in the past, but I certainly did this time. What anyone *thinks* may be true cannot matter. Including me.

Bob is a complete and total prick. He **is**!! Never casually ask him how he's doing:

> *"Life is great, man. It's an endless string of opportunities. It's all good.*
> *"So, the wife left you, huh?"*
>
> or
>
> *"I am absolutely GREAT! Tremendous things just keep coming my way and it's all for the asking! . . . And you?"*
>
> or
>
> *"It just gets better and better. When you realize that, everything just falls into place. It's just one great big adventure, this life!*
> *"So, certainly you're not still unemployed . . . are you?"*

Aaarrrggghhh! His in-your-face happiness is gonna make me choke that arrogant ass!! He's **obviously** found **all** the answers and just has to make sure I know I haven't. GOD!! What a fucking jerk! He can't be happy. He just can't! No one that is happy would intentionally try to make someone else feel less-than. **GOD!! What a JERK!!**

But wait . . . what if he really is happy? What if he really has found the secret to life? I know that he's in some of those find-your-own-power groups. Maybe they *do* have the answers. Maybe *I'm* the prick. I mean, I'm judging him for rubbing me the wrong way. "Judge not lest ye be judged." I guess I *am* the prick.

Bob frightens me. He does. Sometimes he seems so certain of his own happiness it leads me to believe I've missed something. That frightens me.

But there's more going on here: I don't buy it. It comes across like a direct attack. That's what it feels like. I'm pretty sure that's exactly what it is. I'll even be so brave as to say, "That's what it is!"

What of lines like, "Judge not lest ye be judged"? After years of guilting myself with that one, I've come to a new understanding of that true pearl of wisdom. First, every fiber in my being screams to me that Bob is saying, "I'm completely right and you are obviously completely wrong." I now honor every fiber in my being. I think we must.

What I cannot judge or do not have enough information to judge is exactly how Bob's life path is leading him to the perfect and right conclusions for him. He certainly had a hand in leading me to some perfect and right conclusions for myself. I already realize that without him and others like him I would never sit down and ponder what my soul is telling me. If everybody did everything I thought they should do? Boy, would I be cheated out of my own Self-realization.

END
RACISM!

See just how racism is ending.

I'm gay. I don't like having to say that. I'm afraid you're a road maintenance worker in Arkansas that will use that fact to discredit everything that comes from me. I'm afraid you aren't evolved enough to take what works for you and forget the rest. I'm afraid you've said "Yes, yes, yes!" up to this point and now you say "oh, wait, no." I'm betting many of you are doing just that.

I'm afraid that maybe you're *also* gay and haven't been sure about one damn thing I've said, but now you suddenly say, "You go, girl!" What if I were a retired school teacher celebrating my forty-fifth wedding anniversary? What then?

I don't like gay-pride parades. I don't like football. I don't like guys in dresses. I don't like guys that burp and spit "cuz, hey, that's just what guys do." I resent the fact that being HIV-positive was "exactly what they deserve" until Magic Johnson got it. I'm embarrassed by the gay culture. I'm pissed off at the narrow minds that dwell in the deep South and even in North Dakota.

I'm afraid you're pissed off at my opinions. I'm afraid you would have been just fine with everything if only I'd stopped while I was ahead.

If I have something to offer you, something to inspire and uplift you, I hope you can hear whatever that something is. I hope the unappealing wrapping paper does not deter you from receiving the gift. I hope the manner in which the package was delivered to you does not lead you to return it unopened.

If I have offered you something that isn't quite right for you, I hope you will look around and see if there's something here you really do like. I hope you won't just accept whatever's in the box just because the wrapping paper is really cool. I hope you won't sign for a package you don't want just because the delivery boy is cute.

I hope you agree with me. I hope you disagree with me. I hope you see my point, but really think there's a better way to approach it. I hope you've approached so much so wrong for so long that this is the most wonderful thing you've ever heard.

I hope this is the perfect thing at the perfect time for the perfect purpose. Whatever that is.

This book is not founded in truth and will lead you down a path of destruction.

Follow your truth.

This book is divinely inspired and will end your long search for inner peace.

Follow your truth.

I recently took a trip to my hometown to visit my family. There being absolutely nothing to do in this small and lifeless town, we usually end up rifling through countless photos from the so called "good ol' days."

As always, the countless wedding and birthday shots were making a nap sound real good. Until I noticed pictures of my early years. At around age four, there was a brightness and a life about my eyes and the way I presented myself. Then came a most striking revelation. Pictures of me when I was three and two and even one were testimonies to a child filled to overflowing with immense light and happiness and certainty. I can only imagine what it must have been like to be in the physical presence of this magnificent child.

What happened? What happened around age four and five that made me decide it wasn't okay to be who I was? How is it even possible that a light so bright could not burn away any negating thing that dared come near it?

Maybe my mother was right. Maybe those were the best years of my life. And they're gone.

I saw a brilliant, powerful, and loving light. And that light was me. And when I stop and consider it for a moment, that light *is* me.

That three-year-old child was the embodiment of pure happiness. The idea to even question anyone else's thought or opinion had never touched my mind.

Today I am the embodiment of the same pure happiness. The difference lies in the fact that somewhere along the way I began to take a completely laughable question seriously: Is it okay to reveal who I am? Somewhere along the way, about age four, I decided that just maybe it wasn't. By age six I had come to the conclusion that it definitely was not. I have since concluded differently. As much as I have changed throughout the years, there is a part of me that has always remained exactly the same. I have found it to be the purest, most innocent, yet most powerful part of me. The very thing I feared I was missing was always there.

I am the embodiment of a brilliant, powerful, and loving light. You are the embodiment of a brilliant, powerful, and loving light. I think you are absolutely wonderful! You think I am absolutely wonderful! I want to run along the beach! You want to climb the highest mountain! Could we maybe do that?

I'm afraid

you think

the white pages of this book

are stupid

and too mushy and

just some kind of fairyland drivel.

Notice how fear didn't stop me.

x

It's been so hard to look at your face and say the words. I look at you and see someone so in love with me. I look at you and see someone that would surely lose all hope and just stop trying altogether. I see a fragile little child with hope in its eyes and such certainty for a future exactly the way it has always imagined. And now on some little whim I shatter all of that to bits.

I'm sorry. I . . . I *don't* love you. I'm really sorry. I know I've said that I have for such a long time now, but no. No. I don't. I cannot pretend one more second.

The truth is that I *do* love you. I really do. I love you so very much that I cannot bear to deceive you another moment. It hurts just too much. This may look to be very cruel. This may look to be hateful. But the truth is that I'm putting an end to the cruelty. This is the end of the cruelty of allowing you to believe what is not true. This is the end of the cruelty of stringing you along. This is the end of letting you clutch onto something that deep inside you have known is no longer there. Oh, I do love you.

There is something else for me. There is something else for you. If you've listened to the quiet spaces between us lately, you must know that. Our hearts have been carrying on important conversations for some time now. Is it possible that we could go in peace? Could we hold a thought of great happiness for each other? Perhaps not yet. Maybe after the tears and the anger and the confusion. Maybe then?

Ignorance is bliss.

Acceptance is peace.

I took a day off from work and just happened to flip on the TV. Before me was the madness of a high school under attack by other students with weapons and explosives. There were kids shot repeatedly and lived to tell about it and others with their faces blown off. There was mass hysteria and crying and shock and terror. Best friends were shot down right beside best friends. Oh, God, the trauma for such young minds to endure.

So what was all this shit about? It's funny to me that the news reporters said over and over that "no motive for the murders can be determined" yet every kid interviewed said that these guys were completely outcast by the rest of the school. That they were ridiculed and tormented. It was said that one of them yelled, "This is our revenge." No motive? Hello??

Careful who you decide isn't as good as you. It's all coming down, man. I'm sorry, but lives just don't have the perceived value they once did. People aren't buying the burn-in-hell crap anymore. People are less and less bound by fear. Sorry. Every man for himself.

I live hundreds of miles away from what took place today and yet I can feel the powerful energy of it. There is so much to see in this and so many ways to see it.

I feel the overwhelm of the kids that sat and watched or ran for their lives and saw anyway. I feel the mourning. I feel the shift of consciousness and the searching of souls for a higher truth here. I feel young souls realizing they are far more than their bodies.

Empty shells we call bodies fill a room in this school as I write this. I see souls set free. I recognize that they are now experiencing a peace that surpasses the understanding of our finite brains.

I consider the parents who raised the kids who were injured or have now transcended their bodies and I see a need for crying and kicking and screaming and asking why. I see the possibility of great wisdom, great strength, and great compassion on the other side of all that.

What of the boys that created the situation? I recognize deep inner wounds. I feel the pain they must have felt from years and probably a lifetime of ridicule and discredit. What probably started as a desire for basic love and affection unfortunately was turned over to the ego, the source of all madness. They took a basic truth and chose lovelessly. They, too, have transcended their bodies and certainly see a clearer picture now. They probably experience a tremendous pull to return and try again.

It may take stuff like this right now to help us start to see things differently, but won't it be nice when at last we do not?

A sweet older woman who has been a friend of the family since before I was born was sitting on the deck of the country club when a golf ball sailed over the trees, hit her in the mouth, sliced through her lips, and knocked her front teeth out.

Do not attempt to make any sense of anything in this realm.

WARNING: This book contains ideas that suggest there is no hell other than that we each create for ourselves. This book suggests the only thing to choose here is either love or fear. This book contains information that puts you in a position to question who you really wish to be in the face of choice without fear of a vengeful God.* This book makes you wonder what the payoff is if there's nothing to fear. This book treads the dangerous ground of ultimate Truth and in doing so creates an environment which many may misuse to justify acts of violence and hatred. Therefore this book states that you are 100 percent responsible for your decisions. This book may frighten you. This book may need to be closed and forgotten and never opened by you ever again. This book may get into the hands of those not evolved enough to see that there is nothing to fear and that at our core we are all the same and all feel the same and all want love but are afraid of love. This book further suggests that nothing happens by accident and that all things work together for the highest good of everyone.

* Laws of cause and effect will apply.

Are you responsible enough to live without fear-based principles? Are you responsible enough to choose the most loving action even if God will not smite you down if you do *not* choose the most loving action? Do you still need the Commandments to love your neighbor as you love yourself? Is it possible to love anyone because you are commanded to? Do you love yourself? Do you love that you are loved enough and honored enough to be given total freedom of choice and thought and word and deed? Are you responsible enough to handle what the Truth about you is?*

"Yes," "No," and "I'm not sure" are equally commendable responses.

At last we touched. I had longed for him for what seemed like an eternity. And at last we touched. There was an instant flow of energy; a chemistry undeniable. He was big and strong, I was soft and yielding and yet, I took his face in my hands and kissed his mouth. He held his ground and maintained his stance. After all, he was the man here. He could go right ahead and sustain all the walls he wanted. I was exactly where I wanted to be.

Then something happened. He started to melt. He came down to my level. He met me halfway. We fell into each other. Falling, falling, falling. We became one. We entered a state of complete and perfect bliss. Oh, for this moment to never end. Please, please never, ever end.

It was all just too delicious. We remained in this intoxicated trance for one solid, unbroken hour. Not once did we separate. Then we did. We stood in awe at this incredible phenomenon. We had literally lost ourselves in each other. The bond did not want to break. I did not want it to. He did not want it to.

He broke it anyway. He had to go. It seems he was married. After walking away and returning three different times, he finally walked away once and for all. I lost myself in him that night, and I don't even know where to look.

A kiss that melts. A kiss that brings the walls tumbling down. Mmmm. What magnificent joy. What a powerful and altering experience. Intoxicating. Literally, delectably intoxicating.

I gave my heart to this guy. I'm pretty sure he gave his heart to me. We lost ourselves in each other. We lost ourselves. Lost. Forgot. Traded. And as long as the other body is there, no other earthly pleasure is quite as rewarding.

What about when the kiss is gone? What happens when that body is no longer present to place your mouth upon? In case you're stumped, let me tell you. It hurts like crazy.

It always comes back to me. And it was not until it hurt like crazy that I was put in a position to find myself again. After the intoxicating swirl of energy dissipated, after the heart strings were put back in place, and after time healed the wounds, there I was. Right where I'd always been. Needing nothing. Perfectly content. And most important, I had never left. Romantic? No. But most definitely empowering, comforting, and extremely satisfying.

Every "body" leaves. Bodies die. Bodies get jobs overseas. Bodies find other bodies to join with. There is not one body that will not fail you. I say enjoy them. I say have tremendous fun with them. I say fall in love with the Spirit of them. Who knows? You might even find the Spirit of *your* body along the way.

I am not happy right now and I don't feel like trying to be. I feel stupid and geeky. I feel ugly and weird. I just wanna rent some TRAGIC movie and CRY!!

I am just not happy right now and I don't feel like trying to be. I feel stupid and geeky. I feel ugly and weird. I just want to rent some tragic movie and cry.

The world's most codependent dog lives across the street from me. I swear that the owner cannot leave the house for thirty seconds without this animal losing his mind! If he sees the owner walk to his car, he starts howling. And if the owner does indeed run to the store, the howling, yelping, and whimpering will not cease except to catch a breath. And heaven forbid that this guy goes out on a date (like he did last night until 3AM!).

What is this stupid mutt's problem? Has the owner not come back every single time before? What does he imagine is going to happen to him? If he doesn't shut the fuck up, I'm gonna rip his freakin' vocal cords out. I sincerely doubt he's imagining that.

My neighbor's dog barks and wails in an attempt to get his owner's attention. The dog is perfectly convinced that unless he cries and howls, the owner will forget him. Since he makes continuous noise and pathetic pleas and never once tries anything new, this dog is perfectly convinced that his yelping is what eventually brings the owner back to him. In truth, the owner will not be forgetting this dog whom he loves so very much. The owner is ever-mindful of what the dog needs and will supply it, just as he always has.

Maybe a dog is incapable of standing back and looking about the room and seeing that everything is okay right now in this moment. Maybe the dog can't say to himself, "Hmmm. My master has always shown me nothing but care and guidance. It is very uncomfortable not seeing him anywhere, but let me think about this a moment. No harm is coming to me right now. I'm a little bored, but I *could* chew on the fake bone if I decided to. I'm a bit concerned about getting hungry later, but my body is doing just fine right now. I can get through this. I always have before." Perhaps a dog can't do that. But I can. Minus the fake bone.

GOD!! Why hast thou forsaken me??

I am with you always.
(Although I'm much easier to recognize over here in the light.)

God,

I'm losing my faith in you. I've lost my faith in you. I guess that may be a good thing since I sincerely doubt you are a fairy on a cloud granting wishes.

For months I have asked and meditated and quieted my mind and received specific images of who and what you would have me choose in a partner. I'm deducing that this has been an exercise in nothingness. I don't feel hopeful or balanced or enthusiastic. Everything's wrong!

I'm angry at you, God. You have wasted my fucking time for months now. You have led me into a situation I hate at work and you do nothing for me. You give me countless inspirations and no way of making them happen. You suck. The "Absolute," the "Ultimate Truth," is perfectly worthless in this realm! I do not have any plans of sitting around meditating all day. However, I am certain I am seeing things wrong. But how can I fix it? I don't know.

Go with the anger. Go with it.

Just make up your mind that you are going to be angry.

Sit there and be angry.

Come on, be angry, now.

Be angry.

Be what you are.

Be.

When I was eighteen, my father developed a cancerous brain tumor. Nothing tragic had ever touched our family before. But this healthy, robust farmer was now given eight months to live. I watched as the decline headed toward the inevitable death that awaited him and began to question how it would be. It was certain to be an ugly, ugly scene with painful gasping and panic and terror. Oh, what a dreadful day that would be.

I had taken over my father's farm duties. It was the dead of winter and very hard on the cattle we raised. While in labor, a young cow's hind legs became paralyzed. A neighboring farmer said there was nothing to do except leave her to die. What? Just leave her there? My father would have certainly handled this differently! The neighbor insisted he'd been through this before and it was the best way to handle it. At a total loss, I begrudgingly followed his advice.

Death being a big part of my life these days, I couldn't keep this cow out of my mind. I would go check on it everyday. It wasn't dying! Oh, this was horrid! This was cruel. It could barely lift its head and would look up at me in wonder of what was going on. I brought it water and tried to feed it. Perhaps I was prolonging the inevitable.

One day I went to check on the cow and noticed a marked decline in response. She did not lift her head on this day, but breathed slowly and methodically. She looked up at me, I stroked her face gently. Her breathing became more shallow and more shallow until she stopped breathing altogether. She was gone.

I learned something from a cow. A cow removed my fear. I developed an undeniable bond with that animal. She waited all day until I arrived to say thank you and good-bye. She waited all day to show me how gently a soul can be set free. She showed me how we really speak to each other.

And so it was with my father's death. He waited all day one day for me to get home from classes. Not long after I arrived, his breathing became very shallow. It got more shallow and more shallow. He looked up at all of us. We held his hand. We let it be okay for him to go. He stopped breathing altogether. He was free.

"I am a generous and loving human being."

(Oh be serious. It's all about what I can get.)

"I love myself."

(This is stupid.)

"Everywhere I look I see harmony."

(Boring!)

"Everything I need comes to me easily."

(I can't even pay my phone bill this month.)

"Others are drawn to me."

(Yeah, then they look closer and run.)

"I have a wonderful life."

(I hate my life.)

"I love the work I do."

(It might be okay if my boss wasn't such a fuckin' jerk.)

"I get better and better with each passing day."

(I now have so much fat on my thighs, it itches to walk.)

"Life is a tremendous gift to me."

(This shit doesn't work.)

Affirmations really do work.

CRAP, man!
I've gotta get this report done in
5 minutes and this goddamn
computer will NOT stop crashing!
FUCK ! ! !
I'm not gonna get this thing done!

As you ask, so shall you receive:

The computer will not stop crashing.
You are not going to get this thing done.

My first live-in girlfriend was a total nut case. As soon as we moved in together I knew I was in trouble. I'd catch her just staring at the sink, usually before she left to go somewhere. She'd stare at the sink and mumble arbitrary numbers. "54—36—44—84 . . . " Then she'd knock on the sink. Three times. Then once. Then three times. I recognized this as obsessive-compulsive behavior, but she did not want to discuss it or acknowledge its existence.

This disturbing behavior escalated. I later learned, as she was being taken off to the psychiatric ward, that it was the result of refusing to deal with painful memories of repeated sexual abuse as a child. After the trip to the loony bin, she was never the same. She still refused to look at what had happened and spent the remaining months we were together on the couch crying. The crying was so constant and relentless, that I soon joined in on a far-too-regular basis. One day while kneeled down next to this wailing mess, something snapped in me and I discovered that hopeless place in the mind that she existed in. It was time for me to go or else lose *my* mind as well.

My experience of living with this tormented individual taught me much about my own inner strength. When someone you care about is lying on the floor all night long crying and panicked, when you can see that their greatest fears are just about to be realized, and when they have become fearful of being touched, there is nothing you can do. Her pain became my pain and I had to find a source of strength and hope. I even had to find a way to not drink in the emotional turmoil all about me.

As nothing changed more and more, it became obvious that I was doing nothing but allowing her to sit paralyzed in a box of fear that did not exist. I was cooking her meals, doing her laundry, cleaning, care-taking, and enabling. The only chance she had to "arise and go in peace" was if I left the situation. So I did, as cruel as fear tried to convince me it was.

She indeed picked herself up. She at last sought help because she wanted it. She even got on some good medication that handled a host of chemical imbalances. She at last moved out of the madness. She at last found her source of inner strength.

Crap! It's raining! This ruins everything!

Hey! It's raining! This rejuvenates everything!

Every dark cloud has a silver lining.

When viewed from a higher plane,
every cloud is brilliant white and fluffy.

If I say yes, he might get the wrong idea.

BUT

If I say no he might think I'm being a bitch.

SO

Maybe I should try to put him off for a while.

BUT

He might figure out what I'm up to and get pissed.

SO

Maybe I should just tell him the whole story.

BUT

That might come back to make it really hard on Susan.

SO...

Decide anything. Truth will follow.

Fear

Love

AIDS has completely fucked up my life. It has robbed me of the opportunities others my age take for granted. It has weighted me down with all sorts of peculiar ailments. It has led me to hospital beds when my friends were on the ski slopes. It has thrust me into financial ruin as the enormous list of medications adds up every month to what some pay for rent.

That's what I get, you say? Fuck you. You have no idea how I got it. You don't know me. Maybe I'm a woman whose husband was fucking around behind her back. Or an eight-year-old kid. But what if I were a drug addict? Or a sleazy whore? What then?

I know more pain than some will ever know or could tolerate. Do you even know what a tracheoscopy is? How many IV's do you get in your arm every month? If you catch a cold, how many days before you can get out of bed and go to the kitchen?

So after years of rotting away, they finally come up with some medicine that is actually capable of working. So now I'm treading water trying to get back into the working world. I've been gone a while. Many places look at me as having little or no experience. I'm having to start all over. At this stage in the game, that's not real easy.

AIDS has completely renewed my life. It has made it possible for me to be everything I really and truly wanted to be but feared I never would. It has put me face-to-face with every fear I ever had about anything and made me say, "It's either you or me." I chose me.

Before I contracted the virus, I was horribly rigid and walked around with a lump in my throat for fear that I was doing everything "wrong." As certain death entered the picture, I decided, "Who cares?" Who cares what people think? Who cares if I'm too old to do this? Who cares if I'm too young to do this? Who cares who cares?

After years and years of being remarkably healthy, I suddenly hit the wall. I developed a variety of symptoms and had zero T-cells, which we all need to stay healthy. Medicine was not working. Every kind of treatment that was administered to me was only holding me in my place at rock bottom. This was the end. The writing was on the wall and I didn't even want to be in that body anymore. One day around noon, I let go. I dropped the body entirely.

You've probably heard it before, but words cannot describe the freedom. Much, however, seemed the same. I still felt like "myself." I remembered how there is nothing to fear. I remembered how nothing matters. I remembered how any choice I make is not the determining factor in whether I'm happy or not. Then I got a very clear overview of everything I wanted to accomplish in this realm and had not. I decided to return. I made up my mind that I had stuff to do.

It has been my experience that the more darkness I encounter, the greater my capacity for light. Ugliness turns to beauty to ugliness to beauty. The negative with the positive. Up, down. Black and white.

And so it goes...

130